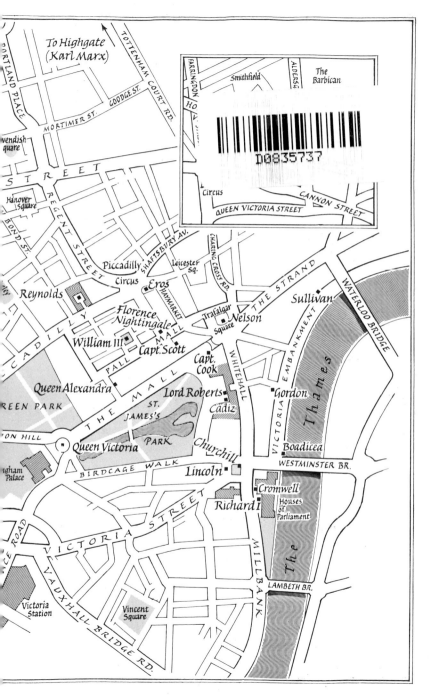

The Immortals

LONDON'S FINEST STATUES

The Immortals

LONDON'S FINEST STATUES

Photographs by
JOE WHITLOCK BLUNDELL

Text by
ROGER HUDSON

LONDON
The Folio Society
1998

FOREWORD

London is populated by more statues than any other city on earth. William III has ridden his horse through St James's Square since 1808, but Mozart returned to Ebury Street as recently as 1994. The vast proportion date from the late nineteenth and early twentieth centuries, and it is most fortunate that Britain's imperial heyday coincided with the age of her greatest sculptors, Victorian masters such as Boehm and Marochetti giving way to exponents of the 'New Sculpture' – Alfred Gilbert, George Frampton and Derwent Wood.

In selecting 'the finest' from the hundreds on display, consideration has been given to the importance of the subject, the quality of the sculpture and its location, but ultimately the selection is unrepentantly subjective.

J. W. B.

Photographs © Joe Whitlock Blundell 1998
Text © Roger Hudson 1998

The right of Joe Whitlock Blundell and Roger Hudson
to be identified as the authors of this work has been asserted by them
in accordance with the Copyright Design and Patents Act 1988

Set in Bulmer at The Folio Society.
Printed in duotone on Lumisilk paper
by Jarrold Book Printing, Thetford.
Bound by Hunter & Foulis, Edinburgh.

CONTENTS

THOMAS CARLYLE

SIR EDGAR BOEHM

Bronze, 1882, Chelsea Embankment

Carlyle (1795–1881) came to London from his native Scotland in 1834 and with his wife Jane set up what was perhaps Victorian London's most famous household at 24 Cheyne Row – a few yards from where this statue now stands. A giant in an age of giants, Carlyle was a historian and historical biographer who transformed his field with his books on the French Revolution, Cromwell and Frederick the Great. He was also a latter-day sage and prophet, thundering out denunciations of and solutions to what he saw as the wrongs of the time in books like *Sartor Resartus*, *Past and Present* and *On Heroes and Hero-Worship*. He attacked the impersonality of Capital and Labour and stressed instead personality, immaterial values and leadership. Latterly his seemingly endless condemnations became irksome, and in this century he has been branded a racist and encourager of fascist dictatorship. It is a pity if that stops people from following George Meredith's advice to 'swim in his pages, take the poetry and the fine grisly humour, the manly independence'.

Boehm has got round the perennial problem which trousers – with their straight lines and flat surfaces – pose sculptors by allowing Carlyle to wear a sweeping dressing gown. The pile of books under the chair in which he sits is a nice touch. If the gossip of the day is to be believed, Boehm died in 1890 while making love to Queen Victoria's daughter Princess Louise, herself an amateur sculptor.

ATALANTA

FRANCIS DERWENT WOOD

Bronze, 1929, Chelsea Embankment

She was erected near Albert Bridge by the Chelsea Arts Club in memory of her sculptor, who died in 1926. As his middle name might imply he was born in the Lake District, though his father was American. After training in Germany and elsewhere, he became assistant to Sir Thomas Brock, the sculptor of the Victoria Memorial (p.28) and Captain Cook (p. 42). He settled in Glebe Place in Chelsea and became a stalwart of the artistic community there, and a member of the Chelsea Arts Club. He was Professor of Sculpture at the Royal College of Art and also taught at the Royal Academy Schools. His busts of T. E. Lawrence and of Henry James are in the Tate Gallery.

Atalanta was an Arcadian maiden from the Classical past, who raced against her suitors. If they were beaten they died. Hippomenes eventually caught her by dropping golden apples on the route. She stopped to retrieve them, which delayed her enough for him to overtake her.

WOLFGANG AMADEUS MOZART

PHILIP JACKSON

Bronze, 1994, Ebury Street, SW1

Leopold Mozart regularly toured with his children, Wolfgang and Nannerl, putting these two musical prodigies on show first in Munich in 1762, then in Vienna later that year. In 1763 they set out on a more ambitious journey, after Brussels and Paris arriving in London in April 1764. They lodged first with a hairdresser in Cecil Court, and within five days a summons had come from George III and his new consort Queen Charlotte, whom Mozart accompanied in some songs. As they were walking in St James's Park a few days later, the king recognised them from his carriage. 'The king opened the window, leaned out and saluted us and especially our Master Wolfgang, nodding to us and waving with his hand.' Leopold was ill later in the summer so the family decamped to the country, to Ebury Street: 'Wherever I turn my eyes, I only see gardens and the finest castles.' They sent out for food but it was bad enough to encourage Mrs Mozart to cook herself. Here Mozart, aged eight, wrote his first symphony. They were soon back in London in Frith Street, Soho. For those not content with a straightforward performance, Mozart and his elder sister would play with the keys covered, or sight-read any piece put in front of them.

Whatever the hotly-debated artistic merits of this statue, the intricacy of its detail shows that the craft of bronze casting is not dead.

PHYSICAL ENERGY

G. F. WATTS

Bronze, 1906, Kensington Gardens

Watts, a looming figure in the Victorian art world, was a very good portraitist, but he also had a weakness for heavily symbolic, allegorical paintings on rather portentous themes. His friend Edward Burne-Jones – a much better artist – put his finger on it: 'He wants to be known as the painter who thought, not as the painter who painted.' 'Physical Energy' was long in gestation, from 1883 to 1904. Burne-Jones reported at one point, 'That horse of his is getting bigger than the world . . . If he keeps on putting more clay and stuff on it, it will go smash through into South Africa.' He spoke truer than he knew, because that was exactly where the first cast was erected, as a memorial to Cecil Rhodes. The one in Kensington Gardens followed two years later, and there is another in Harare, Zimbabwe.

Older generations will remember 'Physical Energy' reproduced on the side of the Energen Crispbread box. Some now find the real statue in the park arresting, while others see it as mere bombast. The rider is listing heavily to his right as he shades his eyes, appalled, one hopes, by the intrusive grey mass of the Royal Garden Hotel. He has what appears to be a saddle, but no stirrups, while the back legs of his mount stretch out parallel like those of a rocking horse. The bronze surfaces of both man and steed are heavily pitted, in an aggressive eschewing of finish and detail, to match the simplified, almost geometrical forms: it is a strangely modern statement from a high-Victorian artist.

PETER PAN

SIR GEORGE FRAMPTON

Bronze, 1912, Kensington Gardens

The statue stands at the very spot where, in his book *The Little White Bird*, J. M. Barrie had Peter Pan land when on his night-time visits from the island in the Serpentine. In writing both the book (1902) and the play *Peter Pan* derived from it in 1904, Barrie was much assisted by the friendship he struck up with the Llewelyn Davies family: five boys, sons of a rising barrister and his wife who was the daughter of George du Maurier, the *Punch* cartoonist and author of the novel *Trilby*. The biggest element in the character of Peter, the boy who never grew up, came directly from within Barrie himself, the classic case of arrested development, but the Llewelyn Davies family acted as a powerful stimulus to his own memories of childhood, as well as being the models for the Darlings and the Lost Boys in the play.

Frampton based the statue, commissioned by Barrie, on some photographs of Michael, the fourth boy, taken in 1906, though of course on stage the character is normally played by an actress. At Barrie's request, the painter William Nicholson, who had designed the costumes and scenery for *Peter Pan*, made the tunic with its scalloped edges and laced-up sleeves, whch can be seen in the photographs and on the statue. The figure itself may lack the disturbing, tragic element present in the stage Peter Pan, but it also largely escapes the whimsy that was Barrie's besetting weakness. The same cannot be said for the base, which is populated by rabbits, squirrels, mice, love-birds, a jackdaw and a snail, as well as a number of ladies, some winged, whose flowing outfits emerge from the base itself and then merge with each other.

THE GREAT WESTERN RAILWAY WAR MEMORIAL

CHARLES SERGEANT JAGGER

Bronze, 1922, Paddington Station, Platform One

A British Tommy reads a letter from home, and for a moment is transported out of the trenches. He strikes the viewer as utterly realistic, dressed for the vile conditions in which he has to fight, a thick scarf round his neck and below that the canvas bag holding his gas mask; his helmet is tilted sideways and back to relieve the pressure on his forehead, and his greatcoat is draped round his shoulders, its collar turned up. And yet the figure conveys a natural nobility and universality that come as an uplifting surprise in an unlikely spot. This memorial, now dedicated to the 3,312 men and women of the GWR who gave their lives in both World Wars, was created by someone who 'knew whereof he spoke'. Jagger (1885–1934) was wounded at Gallipoli in 1915, and again on the Western Front in 1918, when he was awarded the MC. It is one of a number of British Tommies sculpted by him for war memorials (another is at Hoylake in Lancashire), leading up to his masterpiece, the Royal Artillery Memorial at Hyde Park Corner (p. 22). More of his sculpture can be seen in London on the former ICI House and Thames House on Millbank, and his statue of Ernest Shackleton, the polar explorer, stands in a niche outside the Royal Geographical Society in Exhibition Road. Both the Tate and the Imperial War Museum have marvellous bas-reliefs by him.

MRS SIDDONS

LÉON-JOSEPH CHAVALLIAUD

Marble, 1897, Paddington Green

Sarah Siddons (1755–1831) sits by Paddington Church, staring across Westway. She was unveiled by the great late-Victorian actor, Sir Henry Irving. Born into the Kemble family of actors, Mrs Siddons excelled in tragic roles, particularly that of Lady Macbeth, 'the grand fiendish part', as she called it. Reynolds painted her as 'The Tragic Muse' in 1783 and the pose of the statue is loosely derived from that portrait. When Gainsborough painted her, he exclaimed, 'Dammit, Madam! There is no end to your nose' – which, indeed, was true of the statue until it was recently repaired. The poet-banker Samuel Rogers said to Richard Sheridan, 'Your admiration for Mrs Siddons is so strong that I wonder you do not make open love to her!' The playwright replied, 'To that magnificent and appalling creature? I should as soon have thought of making love to the Archbishop of Canterbury!' The painter Benjamin Robert Haydon also testified to 'the awe this wonderful woman inspires. After her first reading [at one of her soirées] the men retired to tea. While we were all eating toast and tingling cups and saucers, she began again. It was like the effect of a mass bell at Madrid. All noise ceased; we slunk to our seats like boors, two or three of the most distinguished men of the day, with the very toast in their mouths, afraid to bite.'

ACHILLES

SIR RICHARD WESTMACOTT

Bronze, 1822, Hyde Park, south-east corner

The story of the various memorials to Wellington in London is a complicated one, but the statue of Achilles, behind the duke's town residence, Apsley House, was undoubtedly the first. It was erected by the 'Ladies of England' and made from the metal of French guns captured at Vittoria, Salamanca and Waterloo. Westmacott based the stance of the Greek hero of the Trojan War on one of the figures in the classical group known as the Dioscuri, which can be seen in the Piazza del Quirinale in Rome, and which shows the 'heavenly twins', Castor and Pollux, taming a horse. Westmacott had become familiar with the group when training in Rome in the studio of the greatest of the neo-classical sculptors, Antonio Canova. Originally Achilles had no fig leaf, and a passing Frenchman described the statue as *'toute nue, toute noire'*. Public opinion soon forced one to be added. (If the Frenchman had been invited into Apsley House, he would have seen Canova's vast marble of Napoleon in the stairwell – *'presque toute nue, toute blanche'*.)

General reluctance to erect a statue of a celebrity while he was still alive was the reason for choosing Achilles, but in 1844 Sir Francis Chantrey's equestrian statue of Wellington went up outside the Royal Exchange, to be followed in 1846 by another colossal one on top of the triumphal arch at Hyde Park Corner. This was removed in the 1880s (see p. 26) and replaced by Sir Edgar Boehm's more modest statue at ground level, which remains to this day. When Wellington died in 1852, the 2nd Duke suggested the money subscribed in memory of him should be spent on putting a statue of him in every market square in the country. Luckily this idea was dropped, and Wellington College was founded instead.

THE ROYAL ARTILLERY MEMORIAL

CHARLES SERGEANT JAGGER

Stone and bronze, 1925, Hyde Park Corner

This is Jagger's best work and London's most outstanding war memorial. There are three elements to the composition: the stone howitzer, the bas-reliefs round its base, and the four bronze artillerymen. The one here, on the west side, his cape stretched out like wings by his resting arms, is equipped with a riding whip in one hand and some harness (with real chains) in the other. The heavy protective gaiter on his right leg shows him to be one of the postilion riders of a team of horses used to pull field pieces. The eastern figure stands with straddled legs taking the weight of the four eighteen-pounder shells he carries in the long pockets of his coat. At the southern end is an officer, his gas-mask bag round his neck, holding his greatcoat in front of him, and with map case, scarf and walking stick. After these monumentally convincing figures, it is a shock to find their dead companion at the northern end, his face concealed by a flap of the coat draped over his body. The inscription underneath him reads 'Here was a royal fellowship of death' – a large fellowship too, with 49,076 Royal Artillerymen killed in the First World War.

These figures (like that on p. 16) are still, whatever reserves of coiled aggression and endurance one senses within them. The stone bas-reliefs, in contrast, are a mass of activity and detail: a man on a field telephone, others serving an anti-aircraft Lewis gun or a trench howitzer, horse artillery, a telegraph pole, a rum jar, a range-finder, a frying pan and cutlery, camouflage netting. Lord Curzon's instant opinion of the ensemble was that it resembled 'a toad squatting – nothing more hideous could ever be conceived'. Today its power and quality are appreciated by more and more who take the time to study it.

THE MACHINE GUN CORPS MEMORIAL

FRANCIS DERWENT WOOD

Bronze, 1925, Hyde Park Corner

Like Derwent Wood's other statue in this book (Atalanta, p. 8), this is a nude figure, but of an idealised youth: David, who has just slain Goliath with his sling, and then used the giant's sword to decapitate him. The sculptor's sources are impeccable: Donatello's 'David' and Cellini's 'Perseus', both in Florence. The contrast between the boy and the Vickers machine-guns which flank him is arresting. Underneath them are canvas bags to collect the spent brass bullet cases: six hundred fired in a minute, ten a second.

The Machine Gun Corps had a short life, formed in 1915 and disbanded in 1922, but long enough for 13,791 to be killed from its number. Haig thought the machine-gun 'much over-rated' and that two per battalion were enough; Kitchener that more than four was a luxury; but Lloyd George saw to it that sixty-four became the standard. The most startling aspect of the whole memorial is the biblical quotation on its plinth:

> *Saul hath slain in his thousands*
> *but David his tens of thousands.*

PEACE AND THE QUADRIGA

CAPTAIN ADRIAN JONES

Bronze, 1912, Hyde Park Corner

From 1846 until 1883 a huge statue of Wellington stood on the top of Constitution Arch at the end of Constitution Hill, at Hyde Park Corner (see p. 20). This was then moved to Aldershot and the arch itself was repositioned. It did not remain unadorned for long, however, because in 1912 a vast new creation arrived. Intended as a memorial to the recently dead Edward VII, it portrays the winged figure of Peace alighting on the four-horse Chariot (Quadriga) of War. Her next move should have been to restrain the enthusiasm of the boy-charioteer but, given the events of the next few years, she must have been diverted from her task, and taken for a ride instead.

The sculptor spent many years as an army vet, so knew his horses. He was also responsible for the equestrian statue of the Duke of Cambridge in Whitehall. Herbert Stern, Lord Michelham, paid for 'Peace and the Quadriga'; there are photographs of his son posing for the charioteer, and of Jones and an assistant having tea inside half of one of the horses. The arch now serves to conceal the ducts taking away the exhaust fumes from the underpass below, no doubt kippering Peace in the process.

THE VICTORIA MEMORIAL

SIR THOMAS BROCK

Marble and bronze, 1911, Buckingham Palace

The apotheosis of the allegorical figure in British sculpture, the Memorial is itself only part of a much larger overall scheme embracing a new front for Buckingham Palace and the building of Admiralty Arch at the far end of the Mall. Whatever the old queen might have felt about being the centrepiece of such a splendiferous arrangement, she would have approved of the choice of Brock, since he had completed the statue of her husband, seated under the canopy of the Albert Memorial in Kensington Gardens, and again surrounded by allegorical statuary.

The top is adorned with a winged Victory flanked by Courage and Constancy, all gilded. Below this golden trio are the queen herself, looking up the Mall, with Truth and her mirror on one side and Justice with her sword (see photograph) on the other, while Motherhood looks at the Palace. On the podium are four bronze lions with Peace, Progress, Manufacture and Agriculture standing by them. Then come two basins replete with dolphins, a mermaid, triton, ships' prows, etc. Above the cascades feeding these basins recline bronze figures of Shipbuilding and War to the south, with Architecture and Painting (see photograph) to the north. Allegories also abound on the gateposts punctuating the semi-circular balustrade and surround to the east, with a leopard, an ostrich, a seal and a kangaroo among the animals standing for West and South Africa, Canada and Australia. Finally Brock adorned Admiralty Arch with figures of Navigation and Gunnery.

When George V unveiled the Memorial, his first cousin the Kaiser was present: all the virtues, qualities, skills and Dominions personified here were shortly to be called in aid to defeat him.

SIR JOSHUA REYNOLDS

ALFRED DRURY

Bronze, 1931, Burlington House, Piccadilly

Apart from his own achievements as a portrait painter, Reynolds did more than anyone else to raise the status of artists in England at a time when they were treated as mere craftsmen. He did this first through the position he made for himself among the country's intellectual élite – Johnson, Garrick, Goldsmith and Burke were his intimates – and then by his establishment, in 1768, of the Royal Academy to hold exhibitions and to run an art school. Originally at Somerset House, Burlington House has been its home since 1868. As the Academy's President, Reynolds gave a series of discourses to the students. He was adamant that history painting, in the manner of the masters of the High Renaissance, was the target to be aimed at, yet the vast majority of his pictures are portraits. In this he was only being realistic about the market in which he had to operate. However, the very success of these is in no small measure due to the 'Historical' elements with which he infused them: the dramatic involvement of his subjects, if not caught in mid-movement, then poised for the next move; his frequent use of a classical style of drapery or props, and of poses derived from antique statuary.

Alfred Drury followed Reynolds's technique, showing him with palette in hand and brush poised to add some paint to the canvas, while he gives his sitter a penetrating look. Such is the power of suggestion that the easel and sitter are automatically formed in the mind's eye.

THE QUEEN ALEXANDRA MEMORIAL

SIR ALFRED GILBERT

Bronze, 1932, opposite St James's Palace

In 1863 Alexandra, a Danish princess, came to England to marry the Prince of Wales. Her sister Dagmar married the Tsar of Russia and their son was the last of that line, Nicholas II. After Eros (p. 63) Alfred Gilbert had received the commission for the monument, in St George's Chapel Windsor, to Alexandra's eldest son, the Duke of Clarence, who died young in 1892. In 1901 the wayward Gilbert went bankrupt and took refuge in Bruges, leaving the Clarence Monument incomplete. Queen Alexandra remained a supporter, sending him money and even asking the Kaiser to ensure his safety during the war. Against all the odds, and thanks to the support of various other ladies in the royal circle, he was asked to design the memorial to Queen Alexandra after she died in 1925, when he was into his seventies. He moved into a corrugated-iron shed behind Kensington Palace where he lived in some squalor but from which emerged this object of surpassing beauty.

Flanked by Faith and Hope, the central figure of Love is about to direct the steps of a young girl, on the brink of puberty, across the River of Life, symbolised by the fountain under the grille at the throne's foot. At the same time the composition has strong echoes of the Passion, with the figure of Love serving for the Virgin in a *pietà*, the small girl in the attitude of a crucifixion and the flanking figures like the women at the foot of the Cross. There are sexual undertones mixed with sacred imagery in this dreamlike symbolist masterpiece, created only a few years before the emergence of the surrealists.

KING WILLIAM III

JOHN BACON & JOHN BACON JUNIOR

Bronze, 1808, St James's Square

Grandson of Charles I, married to the daughter of his uncle, James II, whom he was to force from the throne, the Dutch-born William of Orange is portrayed here as a Roman commander, kilted, armed with a short sword, and without stirrups. The fashion for using classical military dress or draperies for memorial sculptures of contemporary figures began in the later seventeenth century, declined in the mid-eighteenth century, and then returned on the flood-tide of neo-classicism. John Bacon, who had never gone to Italy to study at source, so to speak, was not really at home in the neo-classical mode, and there is more of the baroque about this statue.

It is hard to recognise Lord Macaulay's description of William III: 'A thoughtful and somewhat sullen brow, a firm and somewhat peevish mouth, a cheek pale, thin and deeply furrowed by sickness and care . . . pensive, solemn, severe.' Macaulay went on to admit that the 'phlegmatic serenity' of his hero 'made him pass for the most coldblooded of mankind . . . He praised and reprimanded, rewarded and punished with the stern tranquillity of a Mohawk chief.'

He certainly never earned the affection of his people, though Protestant Ulstermen keep his memory fresh as King Billy, hammer of the Catholic Irish at the Battle of the Boyne. His first priority, however, was always to contain the tyranny of Louis XIV of France. Macaulay again: 'His public spirit was an European public spirit. The chief object of his care was not our island, not even his native Holland, but the great community of nations threatened with subjugation by one too powerful member.' On these grounds alone, it seems churlish that his statue had to wait over a hundred years to be erected.

FLORENCE NIGHTINGALE

A. G. WALKER

Bronze, 1915, Lower Regent Street

In 1837, aged seventeen, Florence Nightingale was spoken to by God, not in her head, but audibly. There was thus little chance of her following the usual route into marriage like other upper-class girls; instead, she took an interest in the care of the sick. Sidney Herbert, the junior Minister for War when hostilities with Russia began in 1854, was a friend and took the bold step of sending her out to Constantinople to try to do something about the appalling conditions in the Scutari base hospital there. His choice was inspired and she returned as the only truly significant hero of the administrative disaster that was the Crimean War. However, to assume that the rest of her life was taken up with nursing would be wrong. She did, indeed, write her famous *Notes on Nursing* in 1860, the same year that the Nightingale Training School for nurses was established at St Thomas's Hospital in London. But her first concern was the care of soldiers and the planning, building and organisation of hospitals. In 1861 she took to her bed and remained there until 1868, suffering, it is now thought, from brucellosis contracted in Turkey. Her invalidism then and later did not prevent her from domineering over and manipulating many who came in contact with her.

When this statue was erected, Sidney Herbert's was brought from Whitehall to share its island site, together with the Guards' Crimean War memorial, seen in the background of the photograph.

FLORENCE NIGHTINGALE O.M.

CAPTAIN SCOTT

KATHLEEN SCOTT (KENNET)

Bronze, 1915, Waterloo Place

Lacking both money and influence, without which it was difficult to get ahead, Robert Falcon Scott had to make his way in
the peacetime late-Victorian Royal Navy. He lifted himself out
of the ruck by offering to lead an expedition to Antarctica in
1901, which got to within five hundred miles of the South Pole,
further south than anyone else had been. The book he wrote
about it on his return, *The Voyage of the 'Discovery'*, made him
famous and decided Kathleen Bruce that he was in the right
heroic mould to father her son. They married, and Peter Scott,
war hero, sportsman and ornithologist, was born in 1909.

In 1910 Captain Scott led a second Antarctic expedition,
which ended in tragedy, though whether because of bad luck or
bad management is still a matter of considerable debate. It is,
however, generally agreed that Scott made a mistake in relying
more on ponies than on dogs to pull his sledges, and in sud-
denly letting Captain Oates go on the last leg to the Pole, when
there were only really enough rations for the four previously
selected. When they finally reached the Pole, it was to find that
Roald Amundsen, the Norwegian explorer, had got there
before them. All five died on the return journey, Scott and two
others when only eleven miles from a supply dump.

His widow made a successful career as a sculptor, earning
the friendship of many of her distinguished sitters, such as
Asquith, George V and T. E. Lawrence. She has portrayed her
husband with his eyes fixed on some icy far horizon, as befits
an explorer.

LORD NELSON

THOMAS RAILTON, JOHN CAREW,
SIR EDWIN LANDSEER

Devon granite, bronze, 1843, 1852, 1867
Trafalgar Square

It was not until 1838 that a competition was held for a national monument to the 'immortal memory' of Horatio Nelson, who had died in 1805. Vanity was his besetting weakness and he would not have been pleased by the delay, but the popularity of the final result must compensate for that. Railton's overall winning design was modified by the addition to the top of the Corinthian column of the statue by the runner-up, Edward Hodges Baily. Of the bas-reliefs, Carew's 'Death of Nelson at Trafalgar', seen here, was the first to be cast. The founders cheated on the specifications for the bronze and were sent to prison. The other reliefs show Nelson wounded at the Battle of the Nile, sealing his letter to the Danish Crown Prince at Copenhagen (he did this below decks, not as shown in the relief), and at Cape St Vincent accepting 'extravagant as it may seem . . . the swords of the vanquished Spaniards which as I received I gave to William Fearney, one of my bargemen, who placed them with the greatest *sang-froid* under his arm'.

The first lions were rejected and in 1858 the great animal painter Sir Edwin Landseer was given the job. The Zoo provided a model which unfortunately died before Landseer had finished, so he bravely carried on working from the carcase: 'Anything as fearful as the gasses from the royal remains it is difficult to conceive.' For a child, no trip to London is complete without being allowed to clamber over one of the four.

CAPTAIN COOK

SIR THOMAS BROCK

Bronze, 1914, The Mall, by Admiralty Arch

James Cook's three voyages were in one sense wild-goose-chases after two geographical conceptions. The first, *Terra Australis Incognita*, the Great Southern Continent, turned out not to exist; the second, the North-West Passage, was eventually navigated by Roald Amundsen (p. 38) in 1905, though it turned out to be of no practical value. But out of Cook's failure to find either came knowledge of the Southern Hemisphere, and of the Pacific in particular, which Europe had never possessed before. Cook was responsible for revealing four unknown cultures: those of the Polynesians of Oceania, the Indians from the north-west coast of America, the Western Pacific Melanesians and the Aborigines of Australia. Yet his origins were of the humblest, and it was perhaps only his being implicated in smuggling off the English coast that forced him to transfer from the Merchant to the Royal Navy, which turned out to be the making of him. It is now thought that he may have contracted an intestinal parasitic disease before the third and fatal voyage, which might account for the signs of stress he displayed on it – carelessness, untypical cruelty at times, and lack of sensitivity.

If his discoveries were the unintended consequences of his travels, they in turn produced their own. By exposing the Pacific civilisations to the diseases, missionaries and traders of Europe, he ultimately brought about their demise.

FIELD MARSHAL EARL ROBERTS

HARRY BATES AND HENRY POOLE

Bronze, 1924, Horse Guards Parade

Frederick Roberts (1832–1914) was born in India, the son of an Irish general, and it was there he made his reputation, first winning the V C as a young officer in the Indian Mutiny, then over twenty years later fighting the Afghans to prevent the Russians gaining undue influence in Kabul. A great bond of affection was created between Bobs and his men. He was sent out to save the situation in the Boer War in South Africa after a string of British defeats, and after the death there of his own son, who also won the VC. His campaigns are listed on the pedestal, together with what may well be the longest and most distinguished set of initials any individual has been entitled to: V C, KG, KP, GCB, OM, GCSI, GCIE, VD. He was also a freeman of nine towns, and was awarded an honorary degree by Cambridge at the same time as Tchaikovsky.

His is the best equestrian statue in London. Volonel, Bobs's Arab horse which carried him on the great march from Kabul to Khandahar, is bursting with energy. His master is dressed in a patrol jacket lined with an Afghan fleece, and with a pugaree (scarf) round his pith helmet. The first version of the statue was erected in Calcutta in 1898, followed by another in Glasgow. Both these have figures of War and Victory at either end and a frieze of soldiery. This reduced version was made by Bates's pupil, Henry Poole.

ABRAHAM LINCOLN

AUGUSTE SAINT-GAUDENS

Bronze, 1920, Parliament Square

President Lincoln is a few yards from his English counterpart, Oliver Cromwell (p. 50). The reasons for the English Civil War are still hotly debated, but the one overriding cause of the War between the States is not in doubt – it was slavery, the 'Peculiar Institution' of the South. Lincoln's position before hostilities is interesting. He believed profoundly in 'the proposition that all men are created equal', but by this he meant equality of opportunity only: 'The Negro is not my equal in many respects . . . perhaps not in moral or intellectual endowment.' His other bedrock belief was in the American Constitution and the Union it underpinned. Southern slavery had safeguards bestowed on it by the Constitution and Lincoln would not pull it down or shatter the Union to free the blacks. The sticking-point for him was the demand to extend slavery into areas previously free of it – the western territories not yet granted statehood. When the Southern States seceded in 1861, it was as much for the Union as for the slaves that he fought until 1865.

As his statue shows, he was a figure of the greatest authority and dignity – six foot, four inches tall – and his words were more than a match for his appearance. The Gettysburg Address is well known, less so his letter of 1864 to the mother of five Union dead: '. . . I cannot refrain from tendering you the consolation that may be found in the thanks of the Republic they died to save. I pray that our heavenly Father may assuage the anguish of your bereavement and leave you only the cherished memory of the loved and lost, and the solemn pride that must be yours to have laid so costly a sacrifice upon the altar of freedom.' The statue is a copy of one in Chicago, and was erected to celebrate a hundred years of peace between Britain and America.

WINSTON CHURCHILL

IVOR ROBERTS-JONES

Bronze, 1973, Parliament Square

It is easy to forget that Churchill was no lifetime Conservative, and that his first political success as a bumptious and very ambitious young man followed his abandonment of that party when he became one of the great Liberal reforming triumvirate with Asquith and Lloyd George after the 1906 election. Today he is particularly associated with the RAF in its finest hour, but before the Battle of Britain he had twice been First Lord of the Admiralty. It was in that post that he advocated the bold attempt to force the Dardanelles in 1915, and ended taking the blame for the Gallipoli débâcle. Throughout his life he was always a keen supporter of the unconventional in warfare, relishing the use of spies and intercepts, special forces and scientific boffinry. During the 1930s, a Conservative once more and out of office, he made a living by his pen, which enabled him to polish those oratorical skills that set the country on fire once he became Prime Minister in May 1940. His great rival for the job, Lord Halifax, spoke of his 'most curious mixture of a child's emotions with a man's reason'. Both were expressed in words and cadences calculated to arouse the nation.

This statue, indebted to Rodin's great sculpture of Balzac, is a bold attempt to summon up the man without using too many of the props – hats, cigars, V-signs – that he himself employed so effectively. But Roberts-Jones's treatment of the greatcoat suffers by comparison with what Jagger achieved with the same garment (pp. 16 and 22), and from certain angles there is too much of the tortoise in the hunch of the barrel-like shoulders.

OLIVER CROMWELL

SIR WILLIAM HAMO THORNYCROFT

Bronze, 1899, The Houses of Parliament

Just as it is strange to find a statue of Boadicea (p.62) in London – the city she sacked – so it seems odd to find Cromwell outside the House of Commons. In 1653 he did after all forcibly dissolve the Rump – what was left of the Long Parliament after Colonel Pride's earlier purge of 1648 – saying: 'It is not fit that you should sit here any longer! You should give place to better men! You are no Parliament.'

John Bradshaw, MP, who had been president of the parliamentary commission that had condemned Charles I to death in 1649, replied, 'You mistake, Sir, if you think the Parliament dissolved. No power on earth can dissolve Parliament but itself, be sure of that!'

Bradshaw was right: after Cromwell's death, the remnants of the Rump came again to Westminster, to dissolve themselves and set the Restoration of Charles II in train.

Lord Rosebery, the Liberal Prime Minister who succeeded Gladstone in 1894, suggested the statue, but met with considerable opposition from Irish MPs. For them Cromwell was a mere war criminal, the perpetrator of unforgivable massacres in their country, though many others had been persuaded of a very different view of him by the advocacy of Thomas Carlyle (p. 6). Rosebery eventually paid for the statue himself. Hamo Thornycroft presented Cromwell 'warts and all', just as the latter had requested Lely to paint him. He holds his Bible in one hand and sword in the other, his hat (a symbol of vanity?) crushed under his arm and his boots pulled right up like fishing waders.

KING RICHARD COEUR DE LION

BARON CARLO MAROCHETTI

Bronze, 1860, The Houses of Parliament

Richard the Lionheart spent only six months of his reign (1189–1199) in England, but that has not prevented him from becoming a hero of Romance. His life was spent either taking part in the Third Crusade in Palestine, being held to ransom by the Duke of Austria on his way home, or fighting in France to preserve the vast tracts of that country which belonged to him. He was handsome, brave, hotheaded, with no further thought than how to raise funds for the next campaign. His Italian sculptor (whom *Punch* referred to as 'Count Marrowfatty') has mirrored these traits in his rather bombastic portrait, which obviously tries to echo the two great equestrian statues of the Italian Renaissance: Verrocchio's 'Colleoni' in Venice, and Donatello's 'Gattamelata' in Padua. The 'Coeur de Lion' began life in plaster outside an entrance to the Crystal Palace at the Great Exhibition of 1851, before being cast in bronze.

Marochetti's other London statues are of Robert Stephenson and I. K. Brunel – the great railway builders – and Sir Colin Campbell (Lord Clyde), who finally suppressed the Indian Mutiny. If the first two had been erected as intended in Parliament Square, and his statue of Sir Robert Peel had not been dismantled in Palace Yard and melted down, there would have been four Marochettis clustered round Parliament.

GENERAL CHARLES GORDON

SIR WILLIAM HAMO THORNYCROFT

Bronze, 1888, Victoria Embankment Gardens

Gordon was a Royal Engineer and fought first in the Crimean War, but made his name in China in the 1860s, leading the 'Ever Victorious Army' of the Emperor against the Taiping rebels. He was then engaged in building forts on the Thames Estuary and rescuing destitute boys. In the 1870s he was again in foreign employ, eventually ruling the Sudan for the Khedive of Egypt, and trying to put down the slave trade there. He was an ascetic bachelor, of profound though eccentric faith; fearless, charismatic and at times unbalanced, with certain similarities to Orde Wingate, the creator of the Chindits in the Second World War.

By the 1880s Egypt was being administered by the British, and a fanatical Muslim leader, the Mahdi, raised the Sudan in revolt. Two British-led expeditions were routed; then Gladstone's government in desperation sent Gordon to conduct an orderly withdrawal of the garrison from Khartoum. He was quite the wrong man for such a job and, instead of retreating, broke his orders and remained bottled up in the Sudanese capital. When he heard that General Wolseley had arrived in Egypt to mount a relief expedition, he wrote petulantly, 'I am not the *rescued lamb*, and I will not be'. Indeed, he was not, meeting his death two days before Wolseley reached Khartoum. Gordon became the late Victorians' favourite martyr, the queen's in particular, and Gladstone shouldered the blame.

Like Thornycroft's Cromwell (p.50), Gordon carries a Bible. His pedestal has two bas-reliefs of four female figures: Fortitude and Faith, Charity and Justice. The places where he distinguished himself are also listed. This excellent statue stood to the north of Nelson's Column in Trafalgar Square until 1943.

HAMO THORNYCROFT, ARA Sculpt

SIR ARTHUR SULLIVAN

SIR WILLIAM GOSCOMBE JOHN

Bronze, 1903, Victoria Embankment Gardens,
below the Savoy Hotel

Visually the bust of Sullivan is something of an irrelevance: it is
the grieving lady who has draped herself round the pedestal,
and in the process allowed her own drapery to slip provoca-
tively below her hips, upon whom the eye feasts. Some years
ago the readers of the *Evening Standard* voted her the most
erotic statue in London. The feelings she evokes and the *fin de
siècle* spirit she breathes are not, however, those associated
with the 'innocent merriment' of Sullivan's Savoy Operas. The
son of the bandmaster at Sandhurst, his musical upbringing
could not have been more correct, broad-based or profes-
sional. He was an outstanding organist, teacher and composer,
particularly of oratorios. He and W. S. Gilbert, a clever and
witty dramatist, began collaborating in the 1870s and their first
overwhelming success came with *HMS Pinafore* in 1878.
A string of comic operas followed, masterminded by their
manager Richard D'Oyly Carte, who built the Savoy Theatre
especially for them in 1881. Sullivan's knowledge of and ability
to write in the style of all the great nineteenth-century operatic
composers gave his scores tremendous breadth and assurance.
It has been said that there are echoes of Weber in *The Sorcerer*,
of Verdi in *The Yeoman of the Guard*, of Wagner in *Iolanthe*, of
Handel in *Trial By Jury* and *Princess Ida*, of Mozart in *HMS
Pinafore* and of Bellini in *Trial By Jury*.

By the 1890s the collaboration was past its peak, but D'Oyly
Carte had made enough money to build the Savoy Hotel and
the Palace Theatre at Cambridge Circus, where he hoped to
nurture English Grand Opera, starting with Sullivan's *Ivanhoe*,
but it was not a success. Sullivan died in 1900.

56

SIR ROWLAND HILL

ONSLOW FORD

Bronze, 1882, King Edward Street, EC1

This lively statue, standing outside the General Post Office in the City, shows how a conventional formula could be reinvigorated in the hands of a practitioner of the 'New Sculpture'. The monument, which emerged in the last decades of the nineteenth century, owed much to French influence and was reacting against the decadent remains of neo-classicism. It aimed to inject energy and emotion back into a discipline that had become formulaic. When allied to the Arts and Crafts movement, it did much to enhance the role of sculpture in architecture.

Hill (1795–1879) had been an educationist before he turned his attention to the postal system in the mid-1830s. It was still very expensive – 1s. 5d. for a single sheet from London to northern Scotland, 8d. to Oxford, at a time when an agricultural labourer might be earning less than 10s. a week. There was massive evasion of charges and the concession of free postage for MPs and peers was greatly abused. Hill proposed one uniform rate covering the whole country, that charges should be based on weight, not on the number of sheets in a letter, and that adhesive stamps should be used. Letters would be prepaid, not paid for on receipt, and envelopes would come into full use. After introduction of the 'penny post' system in 1840 half a million 'penny black' stamps were soon being sold each day. (From February 1841 the colour changed to brick red.)

After a spell running the Brighton Railway, Hill returned to the Post Office and reformed it in every aspect, particularly by introducing promotion by merit. By the time he retired in 1864, 642 million letters were being handled, as opposed to 76 million in 1838. In Gladstone's words, he had also seen his great reform run 'like wildfire through the civilised world'.

KARL MARX

LAWRENCE BRADSHAW

Bronze, 1956, Highgate Cemetery

Marx, a Jewish intellectual from the Rhineland, was just one of many hundreds of political exiles forced to take refuge in Britain in the repressive aftermath of Europe's year of revolutions, 1848. Any hope that he might show his gratitude for the tolerance of his adopted country by fomenting revolution there was soon dispelled by the boom years of the 1850s. But Britain did furnish Marx with many of the materials – in the form of the 'Blue Books', the factory inspectors' and parliamentary commission reports into working conditions – from which he constructed his book *Das Kapital* (1867), the theoretical basis of Communism. He and his family lived in squalid poverty for twenty years, mostly in Soho, and three of his six children died. It was only in the 1870s, when the financial circumstances of his friend Engels improved and he was able to give Marx a regular pension, that the household could move up to Haverstock Hill by Hampstead Heath, and live in decent conditions.

A heroic smoker, increasingly possessed by bibliomania, Marx's public persona was, whatever his private virtues, deeply unlovely. He was a great hater, and anyone he saw as a potential rival was subjected to a stream of poisonous invective. His theory of dialectical materialism, which was to have liberated the masses, led in practice to some of the worst excesses of cruelty and oppression in twentieth-century history – millions were to die in the Gulags and during the Great Leap Forward as a result of 'Marxist' ideologies. It is ironic that this bust was erected in 1956, the year that the Hungarian uprising was brutally crushed by the Soviet army.

OF ALL LANDS

QUEEN BOADICEA *(Front cover)*

THOMAS THORNYCROFT

Bronze, 1902, northern end of Westminster Bridge

Boadicea, 'relished by the learned as Boudicca' in Winston Churchill's splendidly dismissive phrase, was queen of the Iceni tribe from East Anglia. She rose against the Romans in AD 61 after they had ignored her late husband's wishes over the succession, flogged her and raped her daughters. Whatever her merits as a symbol of national resistance to external oppression, it seems strange that she should be commemorated in London, a city she sacked and whose inhabitants she slaughtered. When excavations go deep enough, the black ashes of the buildings she burnt can be seen as a line in the soil.

And, indeed, it took nearly fifty years for the group of horses, chariot, the queen and her daughters to be finally cast and erected below Big Ben. The standing figure of Boadicea looks ready to run out along the chariot pole, a trick which Julius Caesar said the ancient Britons had perfected. The sculptor began work in 1856, encouraged by Prince Albert, who lent horses to act as models. Later Thornycroft's son Hamo (pp. 50 and 54) helped him, but it was some years after Thomas's death in 1885 that a move to excavate a tumulus on Parliament Hill in north London, supposedly Boadicea's tomb, aroused interest in the group once more. Another son, John, a very original naval engineer, paid for part of the cost of casting, and public funding made up the rest. When the statue was erected at last, in Britain's imperial heyday, the opportunity to put a prophetic quotation from William Cowper's ode about Boadicea on the pedestal was too good to miss:

> *Regions Caesar never knew*
> *Thy posterity shall sway.*

EROS *(Frontispiece)*

SIR ALFRED GILBERT

Aluminium, 1893, Piccadilly Circus

While one of the most famous statues in the world, Eros is a contradictory work. As a memorial to the 7th Earl of Shaftesbury (*d.* 1885), an evangelical Christian of the utmost earnestness and probity whose whole life was devoted to improving the lot of the poor – chimney sweeps, children down the mines – the joyous figure of the pagan god of love could not be less appropriate. The delicacy of its execution and of the detail on the pedestal below is also at odds with its surroundings. Hemmed in by tall buildings, its great virtues are lost in such a setting. Its creator, Alfred Gilbert, was a genius, but his art is not a matter of simplified masses; it is small-scale, and can only be appreciated on close inspection.

The blind youth, his torso twisted after releasing his arrow, balances on one foot which rests on a nautilus shell. He seems to defy the pull of gravity and, for once, the spectator is almost convinced that a winged figure is actually supported by his wings. The wonderful helm worn by Eros, adorned with two sets of wings, one facing fore and one aft, contributes to this sense of flight.

The statue was met by a storm of shocked criticism when unveiled. The fountains were condemned for wetting passersby and had to be restricted to the lower part, and all the cups for the public to drink from were stolen. But by 1894 the fuss had died down, and Eros's arrow was lodged firmly in London's heart, where it remains to this day.

THE CADIZ MEMORIAL *(Back cover)*

BY AN UNKNOWN HAND

Iron and cast-iron, 1816, Horse Guards Parade

This French mortar, mounted on the back of a cast-iron dragon and guarded at the rear by a twin-headed Cerberus (the mythological dog who guards the entry to the underworld), was presented by Spain to the Prince Regent. The inscription, in Latin on one side and English on the other, tells why: 'To commemorate the raising of the Siege of Cadiz in consequence of the glorious victory gained by the Duke of Wellington over the French near Salamanca, 22 July 1812.' It would be interesting to know whether the Spanish were aware of the prince's enthusiasm for Chinoiserie, as displayed at the Brighton Royal Pavilion, if indeed it was in Spain that the rather oriental dragon was added. Contemporary caricaturists had a field day depicting clusters of ladies at the foot of what they called 'the Regent's tremendous Thing' or 'the Regent's Bomb [bum]', and passing remarks such as 'What an erection, to be sure!' or 'I could gaze for ever at it!'

The photograph shows, beneath the dragon's claws, the Prince of Wales's armorial crest of three feathers with his German motto – *Ich Dien*, 'I serve' – below. The Prince Regent was Prince of Wales as well before he succeeded to the throne as George IV in 1820.

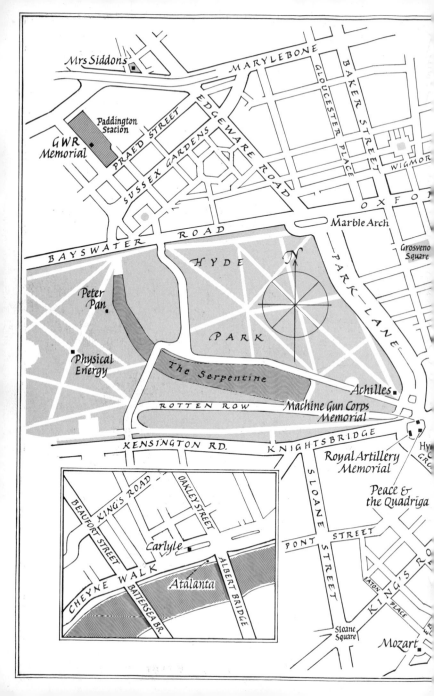